Green Magic:
Algae Rediscovered

OTHER BOOKS BY LUCY KAVALER

A Matter of Degree: *Heat, Life, and Death*

Noise: *The New Menace*

Freezing Point: *Cold as a Matter of Life and Death*

The Astors: *A Family Chronicle of Pomp and Power*

Mushrooms, Molds, and Miracles

The Private World of High Society

FOR YOUNG READERS

The Dangers of Noise

Life Battles Cold

Cold Against Disease

Dangerous Air

The Wonders of Fungi

The Artificial World Around Us

The Wonders of Algae

The Astors: *An American Legend*

Green Magic

Algae Rediscovered
by Lucy Kavaler

Illustrated with photographs and

with drawings by Jean Helmer

Thomas Y. Crowell

New York

For Arthur

Green Magic: Algae Rediscovered

Text copyright © 1983 by Lucy Estrin Kavaler
Illustrations copyright © 1983 by Jean Cassels Helmer

Library of Congress Cataloging in Publication Data
Kavaler, Lucy Estrin.
    Green magic: Algae rediscovered.

    Summary: Describes the characteristics of algae, where it is found, and its many uses.
    1. Algae—Juvenile literature. [1. Algae] I. Helmer, Jean Cassels, ill. II. Title.
QK566.5.K37 1983   589.3   81-43872
ISBN 0-690-04221-3
ISBN 0-690-04222-1 (lib. bdg.)

Photo research by Leonore Morgan

First Edition

Contents

Green Magic:
Algae Rediscovered

1

A World Full of Algae

Have you ever seen a green polar bear? That is not a trick question. If you had visited the zoo in San Diego, California, a few summers ago, you could have seen three of the polar bears turning green. Their backs, sides, and legs had already changed from creamy white to a leaf-green color.

The zoo keepers began to telephone and write to zoos all over the world asking whether anyone else had ever seen such a thing. And sure enough, word came back from nearby Fresno and from zoos as far away as Melbourne, Australia; Auckland, New Zealand; Antwerp, Belgium; and Cologne, Germany. Prize polar bears in every one of them had turned green.

A director of the zoo in Oklahoma City had another startling sight to reveal: Sloths from the rain forests of Central and South America had arrived in the zoo with their shaggy hair colored green.

What could be the reason? Little snips of the polar-bear hairs were sent to a laboratory. There, looking through the microscope, scientists saw green plants so tiny that hundreds and hundreds could go through the eye of a needle. They were growing inside the hairs, which were only a little bit thicker than yours.

These plants are the kind seen in lakes and ponds, and they happened also to be in the pools in the polar bears' dens. While the bears were swimming to keep cool, the plants had gotten into their hair. Once they knew this was happening, the zoo keepers changed the water in the swimming pools. Then they let the bears swim in the clean water until their coats were again a beautiful white.

The sloths had picked up the plants that made them green in the rain forest. Being green is of no use to an animal in a zoo, but in the wild, it can be an advantage. Sloths move very slowly and find it hard to escape from faster, bigger, fiercer animals. When they are the same color as the ferns and vines, it is harder for attackers to find them.

Not only animals are turned green by the tiny plants. The seasonal rains began one December in the hot, steamy Philippine Islands and poured down heavily every single day for two months. Many of the people had to move out of their flooded homes into schools and other public buildings. When the downpour finally ended and the waters fell back, everyone went home. They found that the plaster walls of their houses, which had been white, were now green.

The plant that can grow on plaster walls when it rains and get into the hairs of polar bears and sloths is an alga (pronounced al'-gah). When there are more than one, you call them algae (al'-jee). As the plant always grows in large numbers, that is the name you hear most often.

No matter where you live, you have seen algae. They are the seaweeds in the ocean, the scum on the top of the pond, the green slime on the glass sides of your fish tank. Some, like the ones that got into the polar bears' hairs, can only be seen under a microscope and

Floating algae form a scum on the surface of a pond.
(N.Y. STATE DEPARTMENT OF ENVIRONMENTAL CONSERVATION.)

so are known as microbes; others are a hundred or two hundred feet long and are so big and strong that they can wrap themselves around a large ship and hold it fast.

In 1492, when Christopher Columbus was on his first trip of discovery to the New World, one of his ships, the *Pinta*, became caught by large seaweeds in the Sargasso Sea. The currents in that sea do not sweep in and out like ocean tides. Instead, they go around and around in circles, carrying the seaweed with them. The ship became more and more tangled in the huge algae.

The *Pinta* did escape from the weeds, but other ships had trouble there, too, and in time the Sargasso Sea got a bad name. It was called "The Graveyard of Ships." The Sargasso Sea and the seaweed in it are not really so dangerous, but for years sailors would do anything to keep their ships away.

The same kind of seaweed grows in the waters of the Gulf Stream, where it does not look very frightening. Its body surface is covered with rows and rows of tiny round beads filled with air that work like life belts and keep these weeds from sinking.

The huge seaweeds of the Sargasso Sea and the tiny

Seaweeds exist in a great variety of sizes and shapes. They can look like coral, flowering garden plants, slender grasses, or clusters of berries.

(1. Codium 2. Phyllospora 3. Grinnellia 4. Sargassum)

green algae on the fish tank belong to the same family and are much more alike than they seem at first glance. Algae were the first plants to appear on this earth, and they are the most simple of all. Every other plant has many different kinds of cells, but most algae have only one kind that must do everything. They are not like the plants in your garden with their roots, stems, leaves, and flowers, each made up of specialized cells. Some of the big seaweeds look as if they had all these parts, but what may seem to be leaves and stems are just row after row of the same kind of cell, strung out, one after the other, or bunched together.

Although they have just one kind of cell and no roots, stems, leaves, flowers, or seeds, algae are counted as plants because they can make their own food. That is a basic difference between plants and animals, including humans. Animals have to be given food that has starches and sugars in it already. Plants can take in carbon dioxide gas, water, and ordinary chemicals and turn these into starches and sugars. The way they do it is called photosynthesis (pronounced foh´-toh-sin´-the-sis), and the process needs only energy in the form of light to get it going. That is why you keep your plants near a window. While they are making their own food, plants are giving off another gas, oxygen. This is done by the flowering plants in the garden, the trees in the forest, the corn on the farm, and the algae in the seas, earth, and rocks.

Even though most algae like to be warm and wet, others can endure hot or cold and even dry conditions. This is because there are thousands and thousands of kinds or species of algae, some a little more highly developed than the ones in the fish tank. No one is sure just how many kinds there are, because every time a number is decided on, a scientist goes to a place that has never been carefully explored before and finds another species of algae.

These plants are discovered in parts of the world where you would think nothing at all could be alive. One summer scientists Bruce Parker and George Sim-

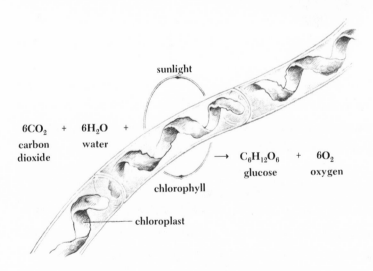

$$6CO_2 \; + \; 6H_2O \; + \longrightarrow \; C_6H_{12}O_6 \; + \; 6O_2$$

carbon dioxide   water   sunlight   chlorophyll   chloroplast   glucose   oxygen

Photosynthesis is basic to life on earth: Plants take in carbon dioxide and water and, using the energy of sunlight, make their own food and give off oxygen.

Scuba divers search for algae under the Antarctic ice.
(U.S. NAVY/JAMES GILLCHRIST.)

mons from Virginia's Polytechnic Institute made a long journey to an ice-covered lake near the South Pole in Antarctica. They cut a hole all the way through the ice, which is eighteen feet thick in some places, to the dark water below. Simmons and a team of scuba divers, fastened by hundred-foot ropes, dived through the hole in the ice and down through the bitter-cold water. And there, through their masks, they saw big mats of algae lying on the bottom of the lake. These were able to grow with just the tiny bit of sunlight that passed through all the ice and the deep water.

When the scientists came up from their dive, they took a closer look at the ice on the top. Deep inside it they could just make out a faint greenish glow. The algae in the ice had been frozen like the food in your freezer. They cut off a chunk and melted it, and the algae defrosted and were alive.

Not all the Antarctic is covered with ice, and those parts that are not, called the "dry valleys," are not any pleasanter. They are as dry as the deserts of Arizona and Nevada, and the climate is much worse. In fact, it is the worst on all the earth. If you were to walk through the dry valleys, keeping your eyes on the ground, you would see nothing moving, no signs of life. But you would be mistaken to take it for granted that nothing lives there. If you picked up the stones and looked at them very carefully, you might see dark-green bands. Botanists, the scientists who study plants, were very excited by the discovery of such rocks and sent them by helicopter to a laboratory at McMurdo

Algae bands in rock from the Antarctic.
(DR. E. IMRE FRIEDMANN.)

Sound in Antarctica. They waited impatiently for the report. The laboratory workers broke up the rocks and looked at the greenish bands under the microscope. Algae were clearly seen.

Just as the Antarctic is the coldest place on earth, the deserts of Africa and Asia and the southwestern United States are the hottest. A botanist who joined an expedition to the Sahara Desert in Africa picked a rock up off the sunbaked sand and found eighty-four kinds of algae growing in and underneath it. The very name "Death Valley" tells you what happens to most living things, but not to algae. Through the many months when no rain falls, they can live just by taking in the tiny amount of dew that appears in the desert each morning.

If you look at photographs of Yellowstone National Park, you will see that there are places where columns of steam rise out of the ground and springs where the water bubbles like the water in a saucepan when it comes to a boil. Such heat is too great for all other plants, but algae can grow in it. They live at a temperature of 167 degrees Fahrenheit. That is the heat-endurance record for any plant in the world. There are so many algae that they color the water of some of the hot springs.

Many people think that algae must be green, because that is the color of so many seaweeds and of pond scum. But deeper down in the ocean or in pools shaded from the sun you will find red algae, and at the lower depths purple ones, some almost black. Brown algae also grow close to the shore, where they are tanned by the sun at low tide, covered with water at high tide. And you can find pink algae, and blue-green, yellow-green, and gold-brown.

Some algae are thick round blobs, and others are tangles of delicate threads or long ribbons, lacy fernlike clusters, wide flat saucers, fluted fans, or strings of beads. Algae are seaweeds, but they grow in so many places that you might also call them rockweeds, soil-weeds, or iceweeds, and since they grow on animals and other plants, too, you could add animalweeds or plantweeds.

A few of the many species of algae have advanced enough to have special kinds of cells for reproduction. But most algae reproduce more simply than that. The single cell just splits in two. One species of algae has been found in Texas that can multiply so quickly that if you started with one and came back twenty-four hours later, looked under the microscope, and counted, you would have one thousand new algae. And each of these would produce another thousand the next day. Most algae reproduce much more slowly. But slow for algae is fast for other forms of life. That is why we have a world full of algae.

The algae found in the Antarctic and Death Valley are not always able to grow there and reproduce. When

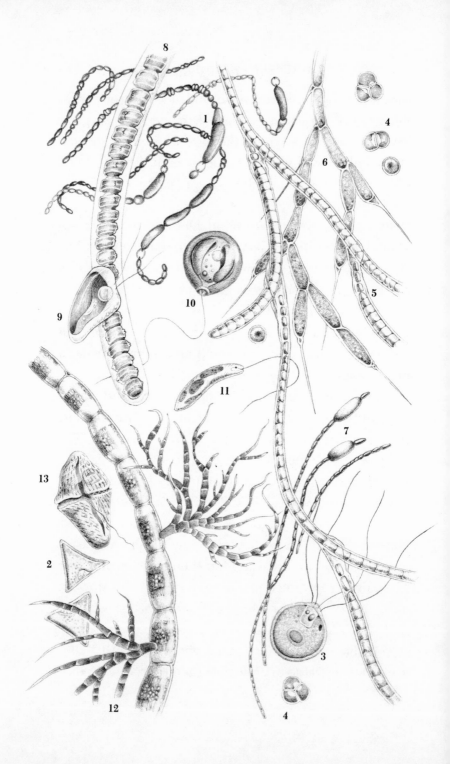

it is too cold or too hot for too long, and when no snow or rain has fallen and the last bit of moisture has dried, algae simply go to sleep. The sleep is so deep that they stop making food and growing. They can stay like this, not changing, for months or years.

But whenever the weather improves and there is even a thin trickle of moisture, they awaken to live again. Unlike Rip Van Winkle, however, who lay down young and woke up old, the algae cells are as youthful as on the day their sleep began.

The microscope reveals the unusual appearance of many kinds of algal cells.

(1. Anabaena 2. Tetraedron 3. Carteria 4. Phytoconis 5. Tolypothrix 6. Bulbochaete 7. Cylindrospermum 8. Desmidium 9. Rhodomonas 10. Chrysococcus 11. Euglena 12. Draparnaldia 13. Gymnodinium)

2

Food Out of Slime

More than six hundred years have passed since the Aztec Indians came from the north to settle in the valley of Mexico and build their great capital city, Tenochtitlán, on the shores of Lake Texcoco. It was in the very place where Mexico City stands today. Over the next centuries, the Aztecs became the most powerful of the Indian peoples, and the population of the city grew.

There were times when the animals they hunted as game and the fish in the waters were scarce and the rulers declared it necessary to find new supplies of food. The Aztecs looked at the slime floating on Lake Texcoco and wondered if they could put it to some use. They had watched the seabirds swoop down to catch some of the slime in their beaks and gulp it down. If it was safe for birds, humans could eat it, too, they decided.

The Indians went out on the lake in small boats and scooped up as much of the slime as they could catch in their fine nets. Back on shore, they threw the slime onto the ground to dry in the sun. When it had dried a bit, they shaped it into loaves and tried it. The taste was something like that of a salty cheese. The Indians named it "tecuitlatl," and it became a popular food.

We know all this because in the early sixteenth century Spain sent troops to conquer Mexico, and the Spaniards wrote down the Indian customs that seemed so strange to them. Eating lake slime seemed one of the strangest. A monk, Toribio, who came to live among the Indians for a time, described how the green loaves were traded throughout Mexico and sold in the Indian markets of many villages.

In 1521 the Spaniards under Hernán Cortés captured and destroyed the capital city of Tenochtitlán. Those Aztecs who survived gave up most of their customs, among them the eating of tecuitlatl. And in time all those who could remember gathering the algae and making the loaves were gone.

In the centuries since then people who read the histories wondered about the sun-dried green cakes, and botanists tried to guess exactly what kind of algae would have made up the slime on Lake Texcoco all those years ago and just how good a food it really was.

In 1964 a Belgian expedition set out to explore the Sahara Desert. While traveling through Africa, they came to the shores of Lake Chad, and as they looked out, they saw a heavy blue-green slime covering the water and gleaming in the brilliant tropical sun. When the desert winds blew at night, they pushed the algae toward the shore, and thick clumps of slime could be seen there.

A few days later Jean Léonard, a botanist with the expedition, went to buy some food at the nearby market of the Kanembou people of the region. Women were selling blue-green cakes that looked like no cake he had ever seen before. When he asked the native seller about these, she smiled and pointed to Lake Chad.

Léonard followed the Kanembou to the lake and watched them scoop up water near the shore in clay pots and pour it into bags of loosely woven cloth. The water drained out, and the algae that had been in it remained. The algae were spread out on the nearest sand dune and left to dry in the sun. Later the women came back and cut the dried algae into small squares, which they took to the market.

The slime on Lake Chad is a kind of algae called Spirulina. Its appearance, and the dried cakes made out of it, seem so much like the descriptions of the Aztec's tecuitlatl that many botanists think that the algae growing today in Lake Chad must be the same kind that grew in Mexico centuries ago. And when a number of them went to Mexico and looked at the slime on what is left of Lake Texcoco, they found some Spirulina there, too.

The Kanembou crumble the Spirulina cakes and mix them with a sauce; sometimes they add the mixture to string beans, peppers, tomatoes, and beans, or to fish, meat, and chicken dishes. But the richer people who live around Lake Chad turn up their noses at the idea of eating slime and say it is a disgusting food. Some of the Kanembou are a little ashamed of eating Spirulina, too, and when they become more successful, they, also, cut it out of their diet.

But even if Spirulina's reputation around Lake Chad is bad, its food value is good. More than half of the Spirulina plant is a good-quality protein. This is a very important part of food, as it gives energy and promotes growth. You get most of your protein from meat and fish. Many of the Kanembou cannot afford to buy meat at the market, but the slime on the lake is always there for the taking.

The Kanembou are not the only people in the world to need an inexpensive, high-protein food. The world now holds about four and a half billion men, women, and children. In many countries of Africa, Asia, and Latin America, thousands and thousands of people go hungry every day. For months, sometimes for years on end, in these countries there is hardly any rain.

The crops wither away, the cattle and chickens get scrawny and stop giving milk or laying eggs. That is what is happening right now, and the populations of these hot-climate countries keep getting bigger. To make things worse, the more people there are, the fewer farms. Men, women, children take up space; they need houses and schools and hospitals. All of these must be built on land that in the past was used for farming.

Maybe we should give more thought to getting food from crops of plants that Americans do not consider as food at all. What about feeding the hungry peoples of the tropics and deserts with algae? A crop of algae needs less space to provide more protein than any other food plant on earth or than animals, say engineers at the University of Texas, who have worked out these comparisons.

Algae contain many vitamins and minerals as well as protein. If you happen to have a health-food store in your neighborhood, just take a look inside. Chances are you will find bottles of Spirulina tablets. A number of drugstores are selling them, too. In the United States, tablets made out of algae are an extra, like vitamin pills, and most of us are getting enough vitamins, protein, and minerals from our regular meals. But in other parts of the world, the alga plants themselves could become an important part of the diet.

For the past forty years farming experts have been looking at one kind of algae after the other, trying to

decide which of them would be best for feeding the hungry people of the world. When they started the search, the ways of the Kanembou were unknown outside of that part of Africa, and the histories about the Aztecs' use of lake slime were ignored as unimportant.

The Japanese took an active part in algae hunting, because their country is so small that there is little land for regular crops. In the mid-1940's Professor A. Watanabe of the University of Tokyo traveled through Southeast Asia looking for hardy algae, and brought back to Japan many samples of soil with the tiny plants in them. In that soil he recognized one of the tiniest of algae, Chlorella. Small as it is—smaller than Spirulina—its single cell is more than half protein, and is filled with vitamins as well. Watanabe put the sample

Chlorella (left) and Spirulina cells (right), magnified many times.

in a box and checked it from time to time. Ten years later, the Chlorella was still alive.

And then two scientists, Jack Myers of the University of Texas and Constantine Sorokin, formerly of the U.S.S.R., came upon a strain of Chlorella that could grow and multiply when the temperature was 105 degrees Fahrenheit. Because the need for food is greatest in the tropics and deserts, clearly this was a kind of algae to watch. Although many other algae can stand the even greater heat of the hot springs, none of them happens to be good to eat.

Soon afterward the news about Spirulina got out, and botanists began to compare this kind of algae with Chlorella. They came out even in many ways. Spirulina is just as nourishing as Chlorella and can do well in water that is dirty and so salty that other useful plants cannot survive in it. An advantage over Chlorella is that the single cells of Spirulina are bigger, so it is easier to gather them and strain them out of water. And Spirulina, as well as Chlorella, grows successfully in tropical and desert heat.

Chlorella and Spirulina can compete for attention, and they do. Both of them could become important foods of the future.

Considering that these algae are weeds, found in many parts of the world, it may seem surprising that the biggest problem in exploiting them as a food source is that it is hard to grow them in large quantities—

and cheaply. Collecting slime in homemade clay pots the way the natives around Lake Chad are doing is very slow. Though the amount of Spirulina obtained in this way is enough for the Kanembou, it is not enough for large numbers of people.

The only way to get enough algae for food is to "farm" them. An algae farm is very different from a farm where corn and wheat are grown, because algae grow best in water. Farmers and engineers tried one plan after the other. Some years ago a chemical company, Soso Texcoco, built a factory on Lake Texcoco in Mexico. The lake was much smaller than in the great days of the Aztec empire, but there was still some water, and it contained chemicals. Every so often the company's engineers were very much annoyed to find that algae got into the machinery and clogged it. They saw this as a nuisance, nothing more. Then the director of the company happened to hear about work being done by a French woman scientist, G. Clément, for the French Petroleum Institute.

You might wonder what petroleum could possibly have to do with algae, but Clément found a link. She was looking for some way to make good use of the chemical wastes that build up when oil is being produced. One of these wastes is the gas carbon dioxide. And algae, like all plants, must have carbon dioxide if they are to grow. Though all plants need carbon dioxide, most would not grow near this kind of a fac-

tory, with smoke and chemicals pouring out. But Clément read the report by Léonard on the Kanembou
and Spirulina, and it gave her an idea. The Spirulina
would be put into shallow ponds and encouraged to
grow by having carbon dioxide pumped in from the
factory. Then the algae would be harvested in a building placed nearby.

When the director of Soso Texcoco heard about
Clément's plan, he realized that what had been a nui-
sance might become a valuable product, and soon Soso
Texcoco was in the Spirulina business.

Americans have also gone into Spirulina farming.

An algae farm in California where the crop is grown in ponds.
(PROTEUS CORPORATION.)

A company, Proteus, set up an algae farm on a barren plot of ground in the Imperial Valley of California. A pond was dug and several strains of Spirulina, among them the kind that grows in Lake Chad, were put in. The Spirulina was ready for harvest, when one of the few things that algae could not withstand happened. A hurricane blew up over the valley and swept away the pond and most of the equipment. The workers saved as much as they could on rubber rafts and started again on higher ground.

If you live near farmland, you know that most crops can be harvested only once or twice a year. It's not

After being harvested at a Canadian farm, algae are spread out to dry. (NATIONAL RESEARCH COUNCIL OF CANADA.)

Dried algae are packed for shipment. (NATIONAL RESEARCH COUNCIL OF CANADA.)

like that with algae. They multiply so fast that they can produce one harvest after another, slowing down a little in the winter, and making up for that in the summer. If you grow corn or wheat, there are leaves and stems to be thrown away. Algae don't have any of these. Every bit of the cell is usable.

When land is too scarce even for ponds, algae, particularly the smaller Chlorella, can be grown in factory buildings. In one plant, designed to show what could be done, Chlorella was put in bottles and then, as they grew, moved into huge plastic containers placed on the roof to get sunlight and warmth. Then, back inside the building, machinery separated Chlorella from the water and dried it.

Even so, algae are not yet being offered to most of the world's hungry people. The very countries where hunger is greatest are the poorest. They cannot build the algae factories, or set up algae farms and harvest the crop and make it into a food. They do not have enough money to pay for bringing in algae grown in other countries.

And so at present algae remain a hope for the future . . . for the time when someone will work out a way of getting this high-protein food to the people who need it most.

3

Cooking with Algae

If you like to cook, you might like to try cooking with algae. It is not as hard as you think. Many young people have done it, to find something new and different to eat, to surprise their families, or as science-fair projects.

The first step, of course, is to get some algae. But don't run down to the shore if you live near the ocean and pick seaweeds, or skim the scum off the pond or the slime off the lake. Sometimes the water is dirty and germs have made the algae harmful. And although many seaweeds are good to eat, there are a few that could make you sick. In order to be sure of using algae that are safe, ask your science teacher how you can get some from the botany department of a nearby college or by writing away to a company that sells algae.

This would be known as a biological supply company. Ask for Chlorella. It's a good choice, because it is easy to handle.

But once you have a bottle or two of algae, what do you do with them? You might be able to follow the example of a high school student who won first prize at the International Science and Engineering Fair in San Antonio, Texas, for her work. She poured the water with Chlorella in it out of the bottle into a big container and let the algae grow until she had a lot of them. Then she took the container to her school laboratory, where she poured the Chlorella-filled water into a centrifuge. This is a machine that spins things around and around and so separates them. She spun the machine until she could scoop out an algae paste. The algae were heated until they were dry and then were ground into a powder. This was added to doughs used to make cookies, cinnamon pinwheels, French bread, and cheese swirls.

But you really do not need any machinery at all to get algae powder for cooking. It is possible to strain the algae at home, using ordinary kitchen utensils. As one junior high school student explained it: "I covered a sieve with a paper towel, put it over a jar, and poured on the algae. The water dripped through into the jar, but some algae remained on the paper towel. I had to try this several times, as sometimes the algae just went through the paper with the water. Then, holding the paper towel firmly in place, I scraped off the algae with a blunt knife. I ground this in a mortar and pestle. Adding a little sugar made it easier to grind the algae."

One simple algae cookie recipe is as follows:

Take two cups of cake flour, half a cup of sugar, a quarter pound of butter or margarine, one small egg, and two teaspoonfuls of Chlorella. Mix them all together to make a dough. Shape the cookies with your hands, or roll the dough out with a rolling pin and cut out circles with the top of an orange juice glass or a cookie cutter. Then put the cookies on a greased flat pan and pop it in the oven, preheated to 350°–375°, for 8–12 minutes. You will have some pretty green cookies when you are done.

You can also divide the dough into two parts, adding a teaspoonful of Chlorella to just one of them. Roll out the two parts of the dough separately, then lay the green on top of the yellow layer and roll them up together like a jelly roll. Refrigerate this for a couple of hours. Then cut the roll into slices and bake. When the cookies are done, you will have green-and-yellow pinwheels.

You can cook with Spirulina, too, just as the Kanembou of Africa do. Some health-food stores are selling a Spirulina powder with the suggestion that it can be added to soup, buttermilk, salad dressing, dips for potato chips, fruit juices, or candy bars made with honey and peanut butter.

When algae were first suggested as a high-protein food, the owner of a vegetarian restaurant in Mysore, India, decided to give them a try. He invited a number of his friends to a meal. They did not ask what went into the green vegetable sauce served with the rice, and the restaurant owner did not tell them. When they had finished eating and declared the meal excellent, he then revealed that the sauce was made with algae and that their meal was more healthful than they had thought. Since many vegetables are green, they had not guessed.

Some people object to green food. "It's all right for lettuce or avocados," they say, "but that's it!"

Bread made with algae can be delicious—if the baker has a light hand with the dough—but guests may refuse to eat it anyway, because of the dark-green color. It may be better to add algae to chocolate pudding; the dark-brown color covers the green, and people accept it happily.

You may wonder why, if algae are so good for you, they are being added to other foods instead of being eaten plain as they were in the time of the Aztecs. But Chlorella and Spirulina, algae that are particularly high in protein and vitamins, do not really taste or smell quite good enough to suit most Americans, who are used to fried chicken, cheeseburgers, and corn on the cob. Algae have a smell of the sea and a taste that can be fishy or salty or, in some cases, be like spinach or dried lima beans. And then there is the problem of their green color.

Algae could be bleached to a pale tan and tinted with food coloring, and artificial flavoring could be added to make them taste like steak, hamburger, scrambled eggs, oranges, chocolate, and other foods you enjoy. But doing all these things adds to the cost, and unless algae are cheaper than steak, no one is likely to agree to eat them.

And so it seems more sensible to add just enough Chlorella or Spirulina to other foods to make them more nourishing without adding so much as to change the flavor. The Japanese who live on islands surrounded by the sea like the idea of eating algae. They have figured out how much Chlorella could be added to tea, their favorite drink, without letting the algae flavor slip in. If just one teaspoonful of Chlorella is put in a pot with four teaspoonfuls of tea, no one spots the difference. The green in the tea does not trouble natives of the Far East.

Green ice cream? We are used to pistachio, so why not Chlorella? And algae make ice-cream flavors stronger: Vanilla tastes more like vanilla, chocolate more like chocolate. The Italians make noodles green by adding spinach. Why not add algae? Instead of pea soup, why not cream of Chlorella? You just have to use your imagination.

As Chlorella and Spirulina are found more often in water than in soil, they are seaweeds. That word is usually used, however, to describe the bigger algae that grow only in the sea and that look more like the plants in your garden. These larger algae are not so suitable for use as a food for the millions. Unlike Chlorella and Spirulina, they need a great deal of water and take up as much space as most other vegetable crops. Still, they are an important food in many countries that border on a sea.

If you had visited Edinburgh in Scotland a hundred or so years ago, you would have seen food vendors on the street, much as you do the frankfurter peddlers on the corners nowadays. But instead of hot dogs, they were calling out, "Buy my dulse and tangle." This was the name for a sweetened seaweed mixture that tasted something like peanuts and that was just as popular as a snack. In Ireland the custom of chewing dried "dillisk" has just about died out, but some of the old men still remember it as better than chewing tobacco or gum. Seamen on the British whaling ships used to eat a seaweed, "laver." It was the only fresh green vegetable they could get during their long, hard voyages. Laver was a welcome relief from dried beef and hardtack and gave them the vitamin C they needed to prevent the dreaded disease of scurvy. Long after the old whalers had been replaced by modern ships with refrigerators to keep vegetables fresh throughout a trip, people in Wales kept on eating laver.

Whenever food supplies are scarce, seaweeds become more popular. During World War II, when the Philippines were occupied by the Japanese army and farms were destroyed, many people were saved from starvation by the twenty species of seaweeds that grow in the waters around the islands. In better times, too, the Filipinos put fresh seaweed into salads, just as we use lettuce leaves, with a salad dressing and perhaps a slice of raw onion on top. And after the meal, everyone enjoys a nice seaweed dessert. The weeds are bleached in the sun, boiled in water, and mixed with melon, mango, pineapple, sugar, and milk.

An even more unusual dish is eaten in the Philippines—when a basic part of the recipe can be found. A certain cave-dwelling swallow glues its nest together by using spit mixed with seaweed. It is hard to reach the nests, as these birds breed in the darkest, most slippery nooks. But every so often someone bold will climb into a cave and find a nest that a bird has left. This is taken down carefully and brought home to be boiled into a soup that is considered a great treat. The tiny twigs in the soup must be put aside, like the bones of a fish or chicken, but the rest of the nest can be eaten. An American scientist once asked for a bird's nest to study in the laboratory, but his request was coldly turned down. Do experiments on a bird's nest instead of eating it? The nests are too rare and considered too delicious to spare.

In Indonesia, bacon and algae are thought by many to be much better than bacon and eggs. The kind of brown algae that caught Columbus' ship in the Sargasso Sea and terrified sailors for years is just another part of a recipe to Indonesians, to be made tasty by the addition of sweet coconut cream. And tourists who visit Burma might not guess that they are eating seaweed when it is mixed with hot chili powder, fried ginger, garlic, opion, salt, and sesame oil.

The Japanese eat more seaweeds than any other people in the world. If you pick up a Japanese cookbook, you will see that seaweed is listed in one recipe after the other. An ancient Japanese prayer for the harvest speaks of favored foods; of course, seaweed is among them.

For hundreds of years it was the custom for the Japanese to celebrate their birthdays on a single day, December 31. The menu for the birthday feast included seaweed, which shows how important algae have always been.

Much Japanese cooking, explains the head of a famous cooking school in Osaka, begins with a thin soup, "dashi." This soup may be eaten alone like consommé, or added to rice, meat, chicken, and fish dishes. Dashi is made with dried bonito, which is a kind of tunafish, water, and the brown seaweed called "kelp" by Americans and "kombu" by Japanese. Kombu is so valued that it is sometimes beautifully wrapped and given as a gift, much as you might bring a box of candy or flowers.

The most popular seaweed is the purple Porphyra. The Japanese algae farmers go out in boats to pick the Porphyra by hand and pile it in bamboo baskets.

Seaweed gathering in Japan. (JAPAN AIRLINES.)

Once back on land, they cut up the seaweed, soak it in water, and then spread it onto a frame made of reeds. This is put out to dry in the sun, and when one side is dry, the screen is turned over.

If you ever have a chance to eat in a Japanese restaurant, ask for sushi and you will see Porphyra. But the seaweed on the plate will not look much like the seaweed in the ocean. It has been dried on the screen until it looks like a piece of slightly crumpled purple tissue paper, and if you were to pick it up, the light would shine through unevenly. Sushi is best described as a seaweed-and-rice sandwich. The perfect sushi recipe is three hundred years old, says a Japanese chef. Start by cooking rice in water with kelp and a mild vinegar and some rice wine. Then take the flavored rice and put it in the middle of the sheet of dried Porphyra and roll it up. Then cut it into slices like a jelly roll. A piece of raw fish may be rolled inside or put on top.

You may never have had Japanese food and may be certain that you have never eaten seaweed, but that is not the case. You eat seaweed without even knowing it. Ice cream is smoother, puddings jell better, pie fillings are thicker, and chocolate milk and syrups pour more easily because a product made out of seaweed has been added.

An old story, sometimes told in Japan, explains how people learned that seaweed can make a jelly. In the

Porphyra

Sushi, a popular Japanese dish, is made of flavored rice wrapped in seaweed (Porphyra).

seventeenth century a Japanese emperor and his party were caught in a snowstorm in the mountains. Looking for shelter, they managed to struggle to a peasant's hut. He welcomed them, but when it came time for dinner, the peasant was troubled, since he had nothing in the house but some seaweed. Still, he had to offer something, so he boiled the seaweed, sprinkled sugar on it, and served it. Some was left over, and having no place for garbage, he threw it out onto a bush, where it quickly froze.

The next day the emperor asked if he could have another dish of seaweed before setting off. The peasant rushed to the bush, but all that was left was something papery sticking to the twigs. He scraped it off and brought it inside and boiled it in water. To his surprise the bits of seaweed in the water formed a jelly. The emperor ate it with pleasure, and seaweed jelly became a popular dish from that day on.

4

Billions of Years Ago

If you were to step by accident on the damp soft cement of a brand-new sidewalk, you would never be able to say that you hadn't done it. Your footprint would show in the cement as it dried. The imprint would last for as long as the sidewalk did. And even if, after many years, the sidewalk got so old and broken that it had to be replaced and the old cement were taken up and sent to the dump, the part that had the footprint might not be ground up. Your children and grandchildren might come upon it long afterward and be able to make out faint signs of your heel or toes. But after a while the cement would turn to dust and blow away.

Rock is much stronger than cement, and there are rocks as old as the earth is old. These rocks were not hard to begin with. They were soft, because the heat of volcanoes had melted them. Elsewhere over much of the earth, seas formed, and the bottom was sand just as it is today. Over millions and millions of years a number of the seas dried up. The sand bottom dried, too, and became harder and harder until it, too, had turned to rock. But before that happened, for many years the sand and other kinds of rocks were still damp and soft like cement, and any living things that happened to fall or rest on them were trapped there forever. Most parts of the cells of these ancient organisms decayed in time and disappeared, but a picture of where they had been remained, just like your footprint in the cement.

Over the ages all the rocks on the earth's surface were rained on and then covered over by soil and uncovered again to be rained on and swept by winds, and these prints became faint. Even when people became interested in learning about the history of the earth and went to these very old rocks, the prints were not recognized as signs of living things. Then in 1911, L. Cayeux, a French rock expert, was looking for iron in the rocks near one of the Great Lakes. He noticed prints of cells that he thought looked like algae and other tiny forms of life, bacteria. As he was interested in metals, not microbes, he did not bother to make a picture of them, but he did mention them in his report. No one paid much attention. When another scientist found this report thirty years later, he simply did not believe it. How could a microbe, which is just a soft lump without any hard parts or bones, leave any imprint?

If you asked most people what a fossil is, they probably would answer that it is a skeleton like the ones of dinosaurs or prehistoric humans you see in the natural history museum. But a fossil can be any remains of an ancient form of life. And so something soft can make a fossil, too. Suppose ice cream slipped out of a cone and dropped onto the wet cement of a new sidewalk. It wouldn't make a clear picture like a footprint, but there would be a sign that something had landed there. People who came across it years later would have a hard time figuring out just what it was. And so you can understand why it took scientists so long to agree that the marks in the oldest of old rocks were made by algae and bacteria.

These most ancient times are called prehistory, because no human beings were there to write a history of what was happening or even to paint a picture of it. But paleontologists, as the scientists who study fossils are called, have to work like detectives who come on the scene of a crime long afterward and search for clues that tell what happened before they got there. Fossils and rocks are their clues to the prehistoric world.

Paleontologists read the rocks almost as if they were

history books. Of course, they cannot be certain that they are reading the prints correctly. But they think they are on the right track. For example, a scientist went to the Belcher Islands in Hudson Bay, Canada, searching for fossils, because the rock there was two billion years old and had once been underwater. There in that rock he saw fossils of what could have been large groups or colonies of algae living together in a mat. But were they really algae? Sometime later he was on a trip to the Persian Gulf and looked into the

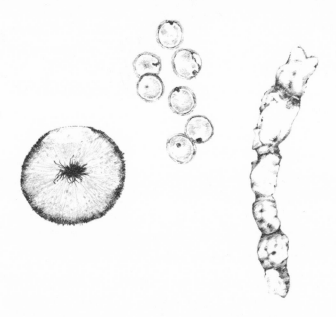

Fossil cells from ancient rock as seen under the microscope (different enlargements).

Fossils of microscopic algae have been found in this ancient rock that once lay beneath the prehistoric sea. (R.C.L. WILSON, RIDA PHOTO LIBRARY.)

shallow water, where heavy mats of algae were growing. He soon discovered that these modern algae and the two-billion-year-old algae belonged to the same species and were in the same kind of mats.

It might seem that everything that is known about prehistoric times would have been learned years ago. But that is not the way it has been. Scientists perfected methods for figuring out the age of a piece of rock only fairly recently. Once they knew where the most ancient rocks were to be found, they began to make discoveries like the one on the Belcher Islands. More are being made right now.

Only twenty-five years ago the oldest fossil was believed to be two billion years old. Algae fossils had been found in rock of that age, and everyone was sure that nothing older than that could have lasted to this day, that life on this earth was probably no older than that.

Then two scientists, Andrew H. Knoll of Oberlin College and Elso S. Barghoorn of Harvard, were studying rocks in South Africa, and they came upon an ancient greenstone. Some of the layers in this stone were three billion four hundred million years old. And as they looked at these layers very carefully, they saw the print of a cell that looked very much like the modern one-celled blue-green algae.

This record for the oldest algae was soon broken. In 1977 J. S. R. Dunlop, a graduate student at the University of Western Australia, was exploring nearby rock formations that were three and a half billion years old. This rock looked as if growing things had once been active inside it. And so within just twenty years, we have learned that life on this planet probably began about three and a half billion years ago.

Can any of us really understand just how long ago algae came into existence? Three and a half billion years is a longer time than we can fully take in. When you study ancient history, you learn about Egypt, the Pharaohs, and the building of the great pyramids. We call it "ancient," but Egypt became a kingdom only a little more than five thousand years ago. What about the time when prehistoric Neanderthal man with thick skull and heavy eyebrows roamed over Europe? That was merely some seventy-five thousand years ago. The bones and teeth of ancient creatures looking like apes in some ways, humans in others, have been found in East Africa. Even these take us back just three to four million years. Let us move to an earlier period when the world was warm and dinosaurs made their way through the swamps. The dinosaurs ruled the world for about a hundred and forty million years, but their era began only some two hundred million years ago. The first algae appeared on earth three billion three hundred million years before that.

The most ancient fossils have been found in other parts of the world, but imprints of algae of a very great age are beginning to turn up in the United States, too— and in so ordinary a place as a road leading off U.S. Highway 89 near Neihart, Montana. In the late 1970s two graduate students, Bonnie Bloeser of the University of California, Los Angeles, and Robert J. Horodyski

Life on earth from its beginnings: Algae and bacteria appeared before any of the other forms and still exist today.

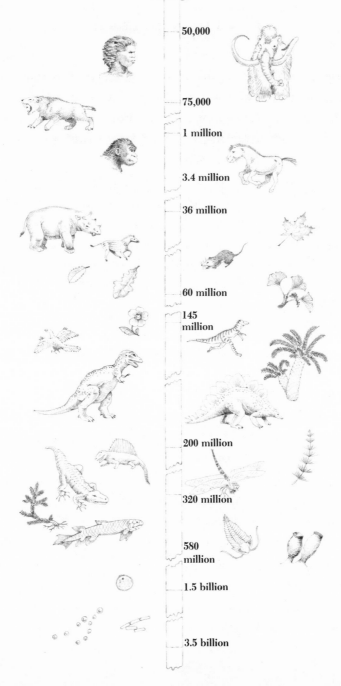

Years ago

50,000

75,000

1 million

3.4 million

36 million

60 million

145 million

200 million

320 million

580 million

1.5 billion

3.5 billion

of Notre Dame University, took a careful look at samples taken from the black rock alongside this road. Inside it they saw fossils of at least four species of algae that were about one billion, four hundred million years old. So far, these are believed to be the oldest ones found in North America.

The ancient rocks, say paleontologists, show that the world was a very cruel place in the beginning. But even in those harsh times, some algae and bacteria were able to live. It was so hard for them that their numbers remained small. Then gradually, over millions of years, the world became friendlier and algae increased in number.

Some of the oldest rock has in it the remains of the chemicals produced by plants during photosynthesis. This is a sign that billions of years ago, in a world different from ours in almost all ways, simple algae were growing in the sunshine just as they do today.

And while they grew, they gave off oxygen. As there came to be more of them, there came to be more oxygen, too. The oxygen went into the atmosphere, suggests Knoll, and helped to prepare it for animals and, in time, human beings.

The study of the history of the world tells us that simple living things changed slowly over millions of years to become more advanced. This process is known as evolution. Algae help us to understand evolution, because some kinds advanced and became complicated and others remained unchanged and primitive in structure.

If you could travel back through time to the years when the world was new, a world with no people, no animals and flowering plants, you would see blue-green algae that looked just the same as the scum on the pond today. By producing oxygen, these ancient algae helped other living things to evolve, but they did not evolve themselves.

The blue-green algae of today and of billions of years ago are so primitive and simple that the cell does not have a nucleus. This is the part of the cell that tells an organism what to do, how to grow, reproduce, and eventually die. Without a nucleus, a cell can do very little. But many of the blue-green algae did not need to do any more in order to stay alive. They were so hardy that they could manage just as they were. Therefore, they never advanced at all.

As millions of years went by, however, some of these algae did need to change in order to live in a greater variety of places. It took a long time, probably a billion and a half to two billion years, but the moment came when certain of the algae cells gained nuclei. And because they had nuclei, they were able to grow bigger. Red, brown, and green algae appeared, with huge branches and leaflike parts to keep them afloat as they moved out into the ocean.

"The greatest single leap forward in evolutionary

history was the rise of the cell with a nucleus from ancestors that did not have a nucleus," declares Knoll.

But even though there were bigger and better algae, the blue-green did not die out. And so today you can see these primitive algae and the large seaweeds as well. It is almost like having a brontosaurus and a modern lizard both sunning themselves in your backyard.

Could algae be a part of the future, too? Someday humans, who have already walked on the moon, may set foot on some of the other planets. We wonder if they will find any forms of life enough like those on earth for us to recognize.

When polar explorers entered the dry valleys of Antarctica, the reports they sent back of the harsh climate and the bare, rocky ground set space scientists to thinking. The explorers might have been describing scenes on Mars or another planet.

Photographs of Mars sent back by a rocket a few years later look so much like photographs of the dry valleys that if you were not told which was which, you would probably guess wrong.

Space scientists joined Antarctic expeditions to see for themselves this "Martian" landscape, and to search for organisms. If any living things could stand the punishing cold, dryness, and bitter winds sweeping down from the ice-covered mountains of Antarctica, then similar forms of life might be able to survive on another planet.

A dry-valley landscape in Antarctica. Tents of an American scientific team are seen against the barren rock. (U.S. NAVY.)

Perhaps at this very moment on another planet algae are trying desperately to cling to life. The atmosphere on that planet may not be too different from the earth's when it was young. As they did here, might not algae help to fill another atmosphere with oxygen and prepare the way for higher forms of life?

5

Green Plants in Outer Space

In a laboratory in Princeton, New Jersey, seaweed is being forced to grow upside down.

This seaweed, Caulerpa (pronounced caw-lair′-pah), is one of the strangest and most wonderful of all algae. Although it is several feet long, it is made up of one enormous cell, with the insides flowing back and forth, forth and back. This cell does not hold just one nucleus, but thousands and thousands. We usually think that an organism with many cells is better than those that have one. Caulerpa shows us that this idea may be wrong.

Despite having just this one cell, Caulerpa is able to live in the warm waters of the world every bit as well as plants that have many cells. "People ask what price Caulerpa pays for having only a single cell," remarks one of the Princeton scientists. "The answer is, 'No price at all.' It does just fine."

It does so well that the scientists are trying to train it to live in space. When it is not being trained, Caulerpa has a stemlike part that lies flat on the ground, rootlike parts that grow down, and leaflike parts that grow up. It grows that way because gravity keeps the roots down and sends the leaves up.

Gravity is what holds you as well as plants to the ground, with your feet down and your head up. And until the twentieth century, no one thought that any plants or people would ever have to live in any place where gravity would not work. We learned that we were wrong when the first unmanned space rocket was sent up in the late 1950s, quickly followed by spaceships with humans on board. For the first time in history, the body was free of the great pull of earth's gravity. Instead, it journeyed through millions of miles of space where there was no gravity at all. Scientists use the term "zero gravity" to describe the condition of no gravity.

The space explorers, astronauts, soon learned what it feels like to be in the cabin of a spaceship at zero gravity. You have probably seen television pictures of astronauts floating about their cabin. On earth their own weight plus heavy space suits would hold them down. But in space, they are light as feathers, pushed to and fro, up and down by the movement of the ship.

It looks like fun, but if the astronauts did not have some way of getting themselves right side up, it would stop being fun very quickly.

To get some idea of how it feels, turn a somersault. You are upside down for just a second. That is enough; you wouldn't like that feeling for much longer. The astronauts have to hang on to the sides of the cabin to get themselves back to their chairs. And once in place, they fasten themselves in firmly. Then, with their heads right side up and their feet down, they are able to do their work, gaze through the windows, and marvel at what they see.

But even though people cannot survive upside down, it was thought that some plants might be able to do so. And that is why scientists Jana Olson Kiefer and William P. Jacobs at Princeton went to work on Caulerpa. "We seek to determine how its growth would respond to lack of gravity," says Kiefer.

But before they can do that, they need to find out what part of a plant cell reacts to gravity. Caulerpa is a perfect plant to study, because its cell is so much bigger than that of other plants. As a first step, the scientists put the Caulerpa in a laboratory tank, turned it upside down, and fastened it firmly in that position. The rootlike part was now up and the leaves were now down. The stemlike part was held so that the side that should have been up was down.

You might expect the seaweed to wither and die. But instead Caulerpa simply adjusted to the change. New rootlike parts began to grow on the side of the stem that would have been up before, but now was down—just as if it had always been that way. New leaf-like parts began to grow on the side that should have been down, but now was up. The plant had turned itself around and was looking just the same and growing just as rapidly and successfully as it had before. The part of the Caulerpa cell that makes the plant grow in one direction or the other appears to be located

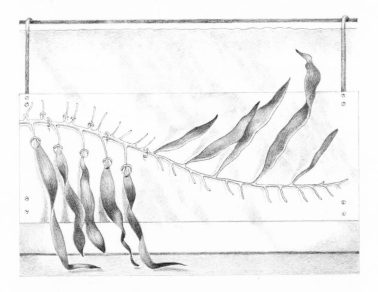

These Caulerpa seaweeds in a space experiment on gravity have changed the direction of their normal growth.

at the tip of the stemlike section where the rootlike pieces form.

Caulerpa will not be sent up in a spaceship. It is much too big, and it is not good to eat. But the scientists hope that once they are sure of what makes the Caulerpa cell grow up or down, they will be able to find it in other plants as well, plants that might be more suited to life aboard a spaceship. And then these plants might be made to grow no matter what position they happened to find themselves in.

The Caulerpa experiments are part of our space program. The National Aeronautics and Space Administration, NASA, is asking scientists to develop a system for providing oxygen and food for humans living in space for long periods. The distances in space are vast. The unmanned spacecraft Voyager 2 journeyed for four years through more than a billion miles of space to fly by the planet Saturn. And this spaceship was not weighed down with humans and supplies. Uranus and Neptune are even farther away, but we mean to explore them and someday Pluto as well.

It has not yet been possible to create a spaceship in which humans could survive a trip that long. But we cannot say that this will never happen. On a summer's day in 1969 Neil A. Armstrong and Edwin E. Aldrin, Jr., stepped out onto the barren rocky soil of the moon. Your great-grandparents would have thought that impossible. Maybe your great-grandchildren will take space journeys to the far-off planets for granted.

"When it comes to working out a system to keep humans alive on long space trips, we are not thinking of what can be done in five or ten years," says Richard Radmer of Martin-Marietta Laboratories in Baltimore, who has a contract from NASA for space research. "We are thinking of what will happen in fifty years. That is what we are working on now."

Space trips with humans aboard have been very short so far. It has been possible to pack everything that was needed. This could not be done on trips lasting many months or years. You have to think of a spaceship as being like a sealed box. Nothing can be added and nothing thrown away.

Just imagine that you are on a spaceship bound for Jupiter. It could not land like an ordinary airplane to pick up food, water, or oxygen. What would you breathe when the oxygen that was in the spaceship at the beginning was used up? What would you drink when all the water and juices had been finished? What would you eat after the last dinner and midnight snack? And there would be another problem, too. Where would urine and other body wastes be stored?

There is a one-word answer to all these questions. And that word is "plants."

To understand why that should be, you have to think about what happens when you breathe. You take in oxygen and breathe out carbon dioxide. Plants, including algae, take in carbon dioxide and give off oxygen during photosynthesis.

You may be surprised to learn that the experiment that showed space scientists what photosynthesis could mean to space travelers was done about two hundred years ago in England. The scientist, Joseph Priestley, who did that experiment had no idea of what use would someday be made of his discovery. He was simply showing how animals and plants depend upon each other. Priestley put a mouse in a sealed glass jar and a geranium in another and connected the two jars with a glass tube. He placed a lamp near the jars. The mouse was frisky and the geranium was growing well so long as the two jars were connected. When he pulled out the tube, both the mouse and the plant died. The mouse died because it was not getting oxygen from the geranium, and the geranium died because it was not getting carbon dioxide from the mouse. Both of them would have died even when the jars were connected if the light had been taken away. Without light the plant could not perform photosynthesis and take in carbon dioxide and give off oxygen.

If you have a fish tank you have been told to put some green plants on the bottom and place the tank near the window or attach a small electric light bulb.

The plants are not there just for decoration, or the light just to make it easier to see the fish. Both are needed to help keep the fish alive. As the fish swim about, they are taking in oxygen from the water and putting out carbon dioxide, much as humans and land animals do in the air. Because the light is there, the plant can perform photosynthesis and take in the carbon dioxide and replace it in the water with oxygen. And like the mouse and the geranium, the fish can thrive and the seaweed grow to a good size because they are together.

The idea of using a green plant to make oxygen and take in carbon dioxide on a spaceship as it does in a fish tank appealed to many space scientists. But for a long time they could not figure out how to make it work. Certainly there would be no room for rows of corn, sunflowers, apples, rice, or even big seaweeds such as Caulerpa. After all, it is hard enough to find room for humans and necessary equipment without adding plants. But what if these plants were so small that a thousand could fit on the head of a pin?

And so space scientists turned to the tiny algae that form the green slime on the glass sides of a fish tank and the scum on stagnant ponds or lakes. Algae are hardier than corn, sunflowers, or apples. They do not need much care, pure water, or cool air. Getting the light to start off photosynthesis is not too great a problem on a spaceship. Algae can use the light of the sun, and when the spaceship goes through places of darkness, electric light bulbs will do. And bulbs have been invented that give off a light even brighter than the sunshine on earth, a light that speeds photosynthesis. These light bulbs produce a good deal of heat, which would harm most other plants. But algae can grow in the hot waters of Yellowstone National Park at temperatures higher than 160 degrees Fahrenheit.

In a laboratory in Pasadena, California, tiny shrimp have been living in glass bottles filled with water, algae, and a few other microbes. They were put into these bottles for an experiment and then the necks were melted shut. There was no way for the shrimp to get oxygen; there was no food; there was no place for the carbon dioxide to go—except for the algae in the water. They were enough.

"What is exciting about this experiment is that these shrimp are still going strong!" said space scientist Joe Hanson sixteen months after the bottles were sealed.

The shrimp are so tiny that a good number fit into a bottle. In another experiment, U.S. Air Force scientists put four mice and a supply of food into a glass bottle connected to an algae tank. The bottle was closed so that the only oxygen getting in came from the algae. It was a space-age repetition of Priestley's experiment with the mouse and the geranium. Only this time there were four mice and trillions of tiny algae. And the experiment was continued for very much longer. The

Shrimp and algae live in these sealed laboratory flasks, each filling the other's needs. (NASA.)

mice were kept in the bottle for fifteen days, and when they were let out, they jumped around hale and hearty. The algae, which had been taking in the carbon dioxide the mice had breathed out, were healthy, too.

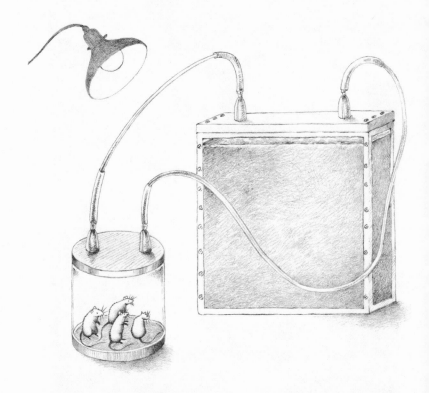

Mice are subjects in this space experiment designed to show that algae can make enough oxygen to keep mammals alive.

Monkeys came next. They also did well, living in a big sealed box with only the oxygen produced by the algae to breathe. And so at last a scientist agreed to spend more than a day and a night in a tank with oxygen from algae only. When he climbed out of the tank, he was smiling.

6

Life on a Spaceship

Algae seem to be the perfect space plant. They give off more oxygen for their size than any other plant we know. But don't think it is easy to make a plan for carrying them into outer space. Though algae are the least fussy of plants, they still need not only carbon dioxide, but also water with nitrogen, magnesium, phosphorus, potassium, and certain other chemicals.

Where could you get all these chemicals on board a spaceship? The answer may not appeal to you: Human body wastes—urine and feces—just happen to have the chemicals that algae need most. And so, instead of worrying about how to get rid of the body wastes of the astronauts on a closed spaceship, why not let algae put them to use?

Think about water. If enough big, heavy tanks of

water to last through a long trip had to be carried, the spaceship would never get off the ground. But urine offers a supply of water that can be counted on.

Urine has been used to water algae right here on earth. Food for both humans and animals is often scarce around Mysore, in the south of India, so algae could be a useful crop. But the farmers are poor and could not buy expensive fertilizer to help the algae grow in quantities large enough to feed them. And so they added human and cow urine, and the algae did extremely well. If it can be done in Mysore, India, per-

An astronaut in weightless condition checks equipment in his closed space capsule. (NASA.)

haps it could be done on a spaceship. The algae would not need all the urine for their own growth; some of it could be treated and made pure enough to be suitable for drinking.

"Use of urine as drinking water after purification gives us some impression of dirtiness, but it is only an impression and the purified water is not dirty at all," said Hiroshi Nakamura, a Japanese algae expert. In fact, he added, he has often drunk this water and found it tasted perfectly all right.

The problem of what to do with urine during a long space trip is solved. And so is the problem of how to keep a steady supply of drinking water. This is a perfect system. What is more, the oxygen given off by the algae as they grow helps to make the water sweet.

What of the other body wastes, which are also a problem on a long space journey? Feces have in them many of the other chemicals algae need. If the harmful substances are taken out of the feces, what is left can be put into the algae tank. As this is taken into the algae's cells to form starches and sugars, there would be no unpleasant smell.

On a really long space flight, sweat, fingernails, and hair might have to be treated and added to the algae tank. After all, algae take many surprising things into their cells. Maybe they could handle these, too.

Food is another problem that must be solved before humans could spend years at a stretch in outer space.

There would have to be a way of growing food on board. As the Aztecs of Mexico and the Kanembou around Lake Chad have shown us, it is possible to make food out of scum and slime. If the astronauts were to eat some of the algae and digest them and then give their wastes back to the algae, the system could go on and on. Everything would have a use.

And it would be easier to take along flavorings to make the algae taste like steak or chocolate or orange or cinnamon than to take the steak, chocolate bar, orange juice, or cinnamon coffee cake.

A number of different species of algae are being considered for space food. Chlorella is a favorite, because it is tiny, easy to grow, loves high temperatures, is high in protein, and has proved itself as a food here on earth. Perhaps Spirulina, which did so much for the Aztecs and Kanembou, might also help keep astronauts healthy. And space scientists have some other favorites.

But even though they may get enough protein, minerals, vitamins, fats, and starches from algae, astronauts are not altogether happy with this plan. They think they might get very tired of an all-algae diet, no matter how well it is flavored. Some variety might be added by growing several different species of algae, but this is not really what the astronauts have in mind.

"There is some hope that it will be possible to grow at least a few crop plants on spaceships for use as food," says Franklin Fong of Texas A. & M. University, who has a contract with NASA. "We would still need to use the algae for food as well as for oxygen and getting rid of wastes. But perhaps algae and higher plants could be grown together, too. We have to first make sure that they would not poison each other while crowded together in a closed tank. In time we might be able to bring in fish and feed them with algae, too."

What we need to do is to build a machine that can recreate on a spaceship the conditions that it takes all of the world outside to create. This is a world in which some living things produce carbon dioxide and others oxygen, some produce chemicals and others use them up; a world in which there are sunlight, winds, and warmth.

And so a machine that brings the outdoors indoors was designed and given the name "photosynthetic gas exchanger"—which describes exactly what the machine must do. It holds plants that are performing photosynthesis and are exchanging one gas, carbon dioxide, for another, oxygen. The main part of the machine is a large tank of water with algae added. The chemicals they need for nourishment are taken from the wastes of the humans on board. Scientists are still experimenting with ways not only to purify, but also to use up every bit of the feces. The best method seems to be to heat the wastes at such high temperature that they turn from their semisolid state into gases. These gases are then sent into the algae tank.

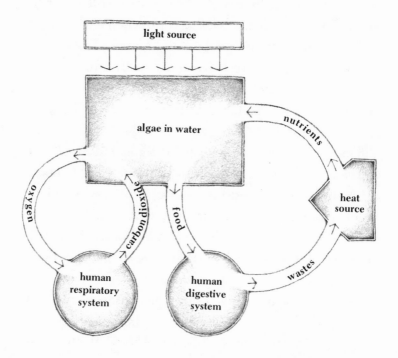

A simplified diagram of a photosynthetic gas exchanger.

A pond on earth gets carbon dioxide from the fish and other animal life in the water. The tank on the spaceship gets the carbon dioxide the astronauts give out with every breath. Tubes attached to the air system of the cabin carry the carbon dioxide into the tank while tubes at the other end carry the oxygen into the cabin. The gases have been exchanged. The tank is placed so that light from the sun or electric light bulbs comes from above, and since there is no wind to move the water, a pump pushes the algae along. Movement in the water encourages the algae to grow.

When the algae have multiplied until there is no room for any more in the tank, some are taken out to be dried and made into food. The younger algae are left behind, as these are the ones that grow the fastest and give off the most oxygen. When they get old, they, too, are taken out to make room for more algae.

Look at the green slime on the glass sides of the fish tank, the scum on the stagnant pond, the seaweeds in the ocean. Plants like these may someday keep humans alive in outer space.

7

Red Water, Green Water

On a warm day one summer, brightly colored patches appeared in the water along the coastline of Maine. The water looked as if it had been streaked with red, orange, and brown paint.

The clam diggers coming to the shore to start their day's work were filled with horror and dismay. They recognized these streaks as the "red tide," which all shellfishermen dread. When it comes, the shellfish are filled with poison, and fishing is over until the water is clear again.

The red tides are found not only along the coast of Maine, but also in Massachusetts, New Hampshire, California, Florida, Texas, Peru, Japan, Australia, India, and parts of Africa and Europe.

People who eat clams, mussels, scallops, and oysters

Hauling in mussels. When a poisonous red tide appears, all shellfishing stops. (MAINE DEPARTMENT OF MARINE RESOURCES.)

gathered during a red tide get sick. The shellfish are poisonous then, because they have devoured the living things in the water that color it red. They are most dangerous when raw, and clams and oysters happen to be among the few animals that people like to eat raw. However, even cooking does not make these shellfish safe. The heat weakens the poison, but does not get rid of it altogether.

The shellfish do not look or act any different, but the more they have eaten, the more dangerous they are. A clam that has taken only a light snack might cause just a mild upset stomach. But because there is no way of knowing how much each shellfish eats, the fishermen do not gather any at all during a red tide.

If you were to scoop up the reddish water and look at it under a microscope, you would see thousands and millions of brightly colored tiny plants and animals. This group of microscopic forms of life in the sea is known as plankton. The name has been taken from a Greek word meaning "to wander." And that is just what the plankton does. It floats through the waters of the world.

Many of the tiny plants among the plankton are algae. Others, the dinoflagellates, are very much like algae, except that they have two tiny "arms" that whirl about this way and that to help them go through the water. These fast-moving plants are most often found in the red tides. Even though they can move themselves, the red-tide dinoflagellates are plants, because they perform photosynthesis, and some scientists consider them to be algae, too.

Most kinds of plankton are not red, and most plankton is not poisonous. Plankton may be any color at all—green, or blue-green, yellow-green, purple, orange, or brown, as well as red. Even many of the red kinds are not harmful. However, the ones that are most often poisonous are red or orange-brown, and when big clumps of them float through the water, they look redder, browner, or more orange than when you see just a few of them. In some parts of the world, the poisonous tides are not red, and the natives there call them the "yellow-green peril."

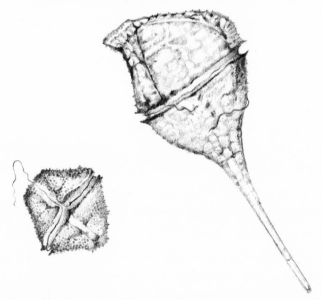

Dinoflagellates, greatly magnified. The thin curly lines are the "arms" (only one is visible in this view of the organism on the left).

Mussels and clams strain the plankton out of the sea-water with their mouths, keeping only the part that they want to eat. Unfortunately, they do not stop strain-ing plankton when the poisonous kinds appear. They like these every bit as much as the harmless ones. And the clams and scallops and mussels themselves are per-fectly well after eating the poisonous plankton. The poison hurts others, not them. Only the people and animals who eat the shellfish get sick.

No one is quite sure of why a red tide appears. Usu-ally it comes in late summer or early fall, after the weather has been warm for a long time and the sun-shine very bright. But that is true in many years with-out a red tide, too. And even stranger is the way the tide disappears. All at once, mysteriously, sometimes after no more than a windy day or two, you can go down to the shore and find that the water is clear again.

But people who live near the coast will not dig for clams yet. They wait to make sure that all the poison is gone. Sometimes the poison is in the water before the reddish streaks are seen, a fisherman explains, and sometimes it is still there after the streaks have gone. That is why in Maine a few shellfish are gathered to be tested for poison every so often between April and October. The first year these tests were made, the chemists discovered that the blue mussel picks up the poison faster than any other shellfish. And so mussels were picked to be the test fish. When the poison is found in the body of the mussels, a red tide is on its way. A warning is quickly sent to the shellfishermen to stay away.

When can they go back? The mussels not only get poisonous more rapidly than other shellfish, they lose their poison more quickly, too. And so when the testers find mussels without poison in their bodies, the word goes out to the fishermen that they can start getting their boots and digging equipment ready.

Some shellfish and fish do not eat the red-tide plankton themselves. Instead, they eat the clams that ate the plankton and get the poison that way. They also are dangerous to eat. Lobsters and some of the other fish are very sensitive to the poison and will die after eating a bad clam.

If you live near the ocean or a lake, you may sometimes find a fish lying dead on the beach. Don't take it home to eat. The fish may have died of an illness that could make anyone who eats it sick. The illness is sometimes caused by the red-tide plankton.

One year when a red tide appeared on the southwest coast of Florida, so many fish died and were washed up on shore that for years afterward the people who lived nearby talked about the terrible smell.

For years scientists have been trying to find out just what poisons are carried by the red tides. Unfortunately, there are many different kinds. In the late 1960s the poisons made by one of the most common dinofla-

Vast numbers of fish lie dead on the beach after a red tide.
(ROBERT PELHAM/MOTE MARINE LABORATORY.)

gellates were identified, and in 1981 the poisons produced by the algae that caused the 1953 "fish kill" in
Florida were discovered. Knowing what the poisons
are like could be the first step to finding an antidote
or cure. Even if one is developed, however, you still
should avoid fish or shellfish that have eaten poisonous
dinoflagellates and algae.

The poisonous plankton does not always color the
water, and the fish that eat it most often survive and
look perfectly normal. And so some terrible mistakes
have been made.

In the eighteenth century explorers sailed across the Pacific Ocean seeking new lands. Ships' records tell how sailors sometimes ate a fish and got sick. One old report describes that leftover fish was thrown onto the deck, where it was gobbled up by a pig that had been taken along on the journey. The pig died. The fish had probably become poisonous after eating a certain kind of blue-green algae that used to grow in those waters and that is known to be harmful.

The fish that had caused the sailors' illness and the pig's death had eaten a poisonous alga instead of a healthful one. This mistake is made more often than you might think. Many fish and other animals have done so.

That is why a fish may be poisonous at one time and not at another. It may be poisonous in one part of the world and not in any other, points out a biologist. Its diet makes the difference.

In 1904 a traveler to a beach in India watched wild horses come down to the water's edge, bend their necks down, and scoop some seaweed into their mouths and eat it. When he came back the next day, he was horrified to see several horses lying there sick. The natives who were trying to help the sick animals told him that the horses always came to the seashore to feed on the seaweed. This time they had taken in a poisonous kind that looked and tasted so much like the good kinds that they had not noticed the difference.

Once in a while farm animals get sick after drinking at ponds where the algae are unexpectedly poisonous.

In the waters around the Philippine Islands there is a seaweed that people are afraid of. It is said to have a strange effect on anyone who eats it. The lips hurt and then get numb. The eater becomes dizzy and sick.

Even algae that are perfectly good may be bad for certain people. You may hear swimmers complain about feeling itchy or having sneezing fits after being in water that is filled with algae. They just happen to be allergic to algae that would not bother anyone else.

Sometimes people want to get rid of algae, even when they are not poisonous. Algae can become a nuisance. This is how it happens:

Although algae can grow all over the world, they particularly like to be warm. Many big electric power plants, paper mills, and chemical factories are located near rivers, lakes, or streams. The water is taken from the stream and used in the manufacturing process, which makes it hot. This overheated water is later piped back into the stream. Conditions could not be better for the algae; the water is too hot for most fish and animals that would eat them. This leaves the field clear for the algae.

One kind of fish and then another disappears. To make things worse, the fish that are best to eat are the first ones to go, and tougher fish that do not make good eating remain. At the same time that the water

Wastes and overheated water from nearby factories pollute this stream, harming the fish but helping algae to grow. (NATIONAL ARCHIVES TRUST FUND BOARD.)

in the stream is getting warmer, it is also being filled with wastes from the factories. This is better and better for the algae, which grow fastest in polluted water. Soon the lake or river is filled with thick clumps of blue-green algae. It is as hard for motorboats to get through as it was for the sailing ships of old to escape from the seaweed in the Sargasso Sea.

A few of the blue-green algae that have a bad smell, look ugly, and may be harmful to fish do best in this warm, polluted water. Those that make the very best food for fish and have a pleasant look and smell are usually not as hardy.

The enormous clumps of blue-green algae get so thick that they keep the sunlight from passing through the water to the algae growing deeper down. These algae die, and their death can mean death for those fish that managed to survive the heat and pollution. Algae take in carbon dioxide and give off oxygen when they grow, but when they die and decay, everything turns topsy-turvy. They give off carbon dioxide and leave the fish gasping for breath. You may sometimes hear of a great fish kill in a lake where the fish died because they could not get enough oxygen. The algae were dying, too, but few people bothered to mention that.

It is not like that in the oceans, however, not even in tropical seas where the temperature is high. The seas are so vast that there is more than enough room for algae and other plankton.

And only a few kinds become a nuisance or are harmful. By far the largest number of species making up the plankton are good. The plankton in the oceans is one of the most valuable foods in all the world— both for people living along the coasts and for fish. In parts of the ocean where plankton is plentiful, fish are plentiful. When plankton is scarce, fish die out or move away. Plankton is so important to all higher forms of life in the sea that scientists are sug-

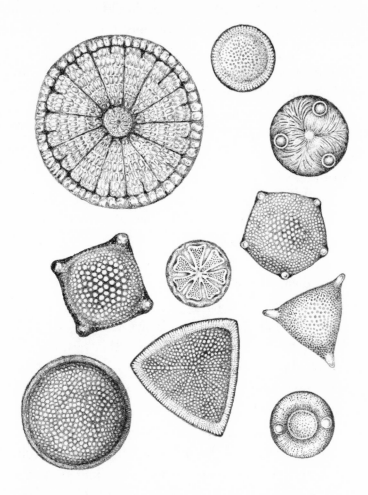

Enlarged views of diatoms, the most common algae among the plankton, show a variety of elaborate patterns.

gesting that plankton be carried in large jars on board ships and dumped in places where it is needed. Fish soon would find their way to so tasty a supply of food. As plankton is healthful, the fish would grow big and multiply. People could eat not only the fish, but the plankton as well.

Scientists at the Scripps Institution of Oceanography in California take plankton so seriously that a way to find it by satellite has been worked out. A satellite is an object sent up into space and left there. From its position far above the earth, it sends back valuable information on what goes on here. The equipment on the satellite recognizes the places where there is a lot of plankton by the color of the water. Fisheries could be built in these places.

In the Far East, many people think plankton makes a tasty dish. The natives of Thailand strain the sea through very fine nets, as the organisms are so tiny they would fall through the holes of a big strainer. The plankton is ground into a paste that tastes something like fish paste and is added to rice to make it more nourishing. Far from being poisonous, most plankton is filled with protein and vitamins.

Some scientists think that plankton could become an important food of the future, along with Chlorella and Spirulina, if an inexpensive way could be found for straining large enough amounts out of the vastness of the sea.

Algae are the strangest of plants. A few are deadly; a few are a nuisance. But most are a supply of food and oxygen. If you were to make two columns, one listing the ways algae are harmful and the other the ways they are helpful, the helpful column would be the longest by far. There are many more good algae than bad.

8

Magical Algae

Could we make the desert green? Could the desert bloom?

Over the ages countless people have dreamed that this could be done as they struggled to find food on the dry barren soil of the vast deserts of the world. But until recently no one had thought that the desert could be made green with algae.

Instead there has been one try after the other to grow higher plants, such as wheat or barley, in the desert. Farmers have had to shield the young seedlings from the sun and to water them constantly to keep them alive in the heat. Some deserts border on the sea, but the salt water cannot be given to crop plants. Other deserts have streams of water far beneath the soil, but this is also usually salty or is polluted, and the plants cannot stand that either. And so the desert farmers have to share their scarce drops of good water with their crops.

The primitive algae are not demanding. Being seaweeds, they can grow in salt water. They are not harmed by dirt or pollution. Give them even the poorest kind of water and they will grow in the desert. The climate is good for them. Every day is hot, and many species of algae do best at high temperatures. The brilliance of the sun shining on the sand has driven people who were lost in the desert mad. The rays are so powerful that they destroy most plants. But not algae, which love the strong sunlight as they perform photosynthesis and grow.

A crop of algae could be grown in the desert in ponds of dirty water. It could be made into food. But there is yet another way in which algae could make the desert green, and it is even more important. Algae can turn bad water into good so that it could be used for crops of corn, wheat, or beans.

This was discovered in a roundabout way. The nitrogen and other chemicals that algae need are hard to find in the desert. They could be brought in from other countries, but this is expensive, and many of the countries that most need food and pure water have little money to spare. So scientists began to look for a way of getting these chemicals that would not cost anything. And they came upon the same method that space scien-

At an experimental project in Israel, algae are being used to purify sewage-filled water. Here, a scientist checks a sample. (ISRAEL CONSULATE GENERAL.)

tists were developing. It works as well on earth as on spaceships.

And so an experiment that sounded repulsive to some people but that made a lot of sense was carried out by William J. Oswald and Harold B. Gotaas at the University of California at Berkeley. Fresh manure was gathered from animal pens and put into shallow ponds where algae had been "planted."

An earlier group of algae users, the Aztecs, did the same thing. The Aztecs in Tenochtitlán faced the same

problem we have today in our big cities. They needed
to find a way of getting rid of their body wastes, sewage,
and garbage. The nearest place to dump them and
get them off the streets was in Lake Texcoco. This
did not stop the Aztecs from taking the algae in the
water for food. You might wonder that they would
be able to eat the algae that grew in the lake with
all that sewage without getting sick, but the histories
tell us that the tecuitlatl eaters were healthy.

The Aztecs had stumbled on a very good method
for getting rid of sewage, producing food, and making
dirty lake water pure, all at the same time. It was based
on algae and photosynthesis. In their system the hot
Mexican sun provided the light algae need to start the
process. The cooking fires of the Aztecs provided the
carbon dioxide. Their sewage provided the nitrogen
and other chemicals. With everything they needed
available, the algae began to grow. Like all green
plants, as they grew, they gave off oxygen. It happens
that oxygen is the very thing that makes polluted water
become pure. And though it is true that any plant could
offer this oxygen, roses, cabbages, and cherry trees
could not live in such bad water. Only the primitive
algae can. And so algae could mean a great deal to
people today living in desert countries, such as Israel,
where pure water is so scarce.

In the tropics, which are both hot and steamy, there
is a lot of water. But in the poorer parts, very little

of it is good to drink. In some places there are so few buildings with bathrooms that people use the streams and rivers instead. They bathe in this water and wash their clothes in it. After a while the water smells bad and looks dirty. In many of these countries, too, food is needed as desperately as water, by animals as well as humans. Animals will accept algae gladly, which is not always true of humans in countries where seaweeds are not a common food.

The fact that animals like algae can be put to use. It suggests a way of getting food that humans also will like, by means of algae. Scientists found out about this by studying records of farming customs of ancient times. They learned that algae had been "farmed" in many countries as a kind of animal feed. Fish and ducks were brought into ponds where algae were grown. The farmers and their families did not eat the algae. Instead, the fish and birds ate it and then they were eaten.

The algae farmers of early times may have gotten the idea of feeding fish with algae by seeing what happened in nature. The yellow-eyed mullet, which lives in the warm waters of the bays around southwestern Australia, for instance, gets its energy from algae. We know this because a scientist examined the stomachs of thousands of these fish and found just one kind of food inside, and that was green algae.

Fried catfish is not everyone's idea of a treat, but it is a very popular dish in many southern states. If you want to find out what the catfish eat, take a look at a tropical fish tank at an aquarium or pet store. There at the bottom you will see catfish swimming. These ugly fish are put into the tank because they eat the algae that would otherwise cover the tank with a heavy green slime.

The armored catfish of Panama have flat mouths and teeth shaped like those on your comb. With these teeth they scrape algae off the rocks on the stream bottom. When scientist Mary E. Power of the University of Washington counted the catfish in a number of large waterways in Panama, she found that many were in pools that lay in the sun, and few were in shaded pools. Catfish do not particularly like the sun, but algae do. One male catfish was captured and kept without food for several days. Then he was turned loose in a dark pool. The fish swam along the bottom for a while and then, still hungry, swam all the way to a sunnier pool where the algae grew in thick clumps.

In some rivers of Poland, two kinds of fish live together peacefully. One is a vegetarian and eats only algae, and the other, a species of trout, eats only the tiny animals among the plankton. And so, though food is scarce in the stream, there is enough for them both.

Every year during the rainy season in India the Ganges River rises and the algae multiply. Tiny shellfish swim to feast on the algae. Soon the Bombay duck, which is a fish, not a duck at all, appears there, too, attracted by an algae meal. Each June when the rains begin, the fishermen who live near the Ganges prepare their nets and fishing poles and watch the water become green with the algae that will bring the tiny shellfish and the Bombay duck. If there were no algae, they would have a hard time finding shellfish and fish.

One thing leads to another, as in a set of "magic boxes." You start with just one box. But when you open it, there is another box inside. You open that and inside there is another, still smaller; and then another, still smaller, inside of that; and so on.

One day a scientist performed that same trick with a fish instead of a box. He caught the fish in the river and cut open its stomach. Inside he found tinier fish, herring. He cut open the stomachs of these herring, and there inside were still tinier creatures. Again he examined the stomachs of these tiniest fish. Something greenish was inside. By now he was using a microscope, because what lay inside the tiny stomachs was tinier still. Under the microscope he recognized algae.

Scientists do not call this the "magic box," but say it is a "food chain," and algae are the first link. The ancient Chinese, who were among the first people to grow algae in their fish ponds, had a saying: Big fish eat little fish, little fish eat shrimp, shrimp eat mud.

They are describing a food chain, because algae grow in the mud.

Antarctic explorers have spotted forty-four species

of penguins and other birds, six of seals, and fourteen of whales in the seas around that continent, along with many fishes, both large and small. All of them eat krill, which are tiny shellfish floating in the waters. The huge whale population takes in forty-three million tons of krill a year. Penguins eat another fourteen mil-

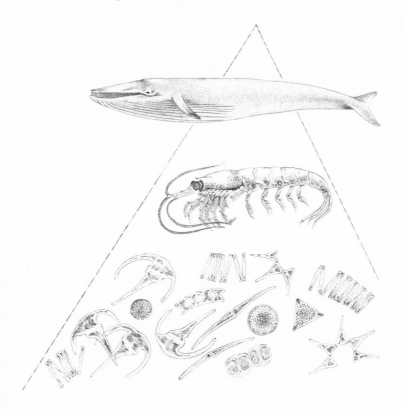

A food chain. Whales gulp in tiny krill (shellfish) by the thousands; the krill in turn live on microscopic algae. (Sizes not to scale.)

lion tons. You can see just how important krill are to these creatures of the icy polar seas. And what do krill eat? They eat algae, of course.

It is not surprising that many fishermen and farmers believe that algae have a great future as an animal feed. Algae have been fed to chickens, pigs, sheep, and cattle. These animals gained weight, were healthy, and seemed to have no fault to find with this diet. Most animals in the wild will eat seaweed if it comes their way. One German scientist went so far as to cut into a cockroach. Algae were there. They have also been found in the stomachs of wild goats, deer, boar, rats, and frogs.

Hens given feed with Spirulina in it have laid eggs with yolks of so bright an orange color that it startled the farmer the first time he tried one for breakfast.

This farmer was not the only person to be surprised by what an algae diet could do. Soso Texcoco, the Mexican producers of Spirulina, shipped some to Japan, where they were bought by a man who raised tropical fish. A few days later, when looking over his fish to decide which to offer to his best customers, the owner saw that those fish that had eaten Spirulina had turned a particularly beautiful shade of blue. When the customers came, they thought these fish were even more rare and unusual than any they had bought in the past.

It seems like magic for algae to turn tropical fish blue and egg yolks orange, but there is a scientific reason for this "magic." Within their single cell these primitive plants have chemicals that can make several different colors. Inside the bodies of the tropical fish in Japan a reaction took place with the blue group of chemicals. In the hens, on the other hand, the reaction was with the orange.

9

Making the Crops Grow

An Ohio high school student was trying to find a good project to enter in a science fair a few years ago. She was interested in farming and began to look into the problems farmers have of growing crops on land that is not fertile. It is possible, of course, for them to buy fertilizers to add to the soil. But fertilizers are expensive, partly because the factories that make them need to use a great deal of costly oil and gas energy.

But what if there were a cheaper and easier way of making the soil fertile? asked the student, Elizabeth Bryenton. She began to look for something in nature that would work, and in the course of her reading, she learned about algae. And so she took fifteen different kinds of algae and experimented with them to see which ones would make the best fertilizer. She did not have any fancy equipment, but made a kind of laboratory at home. Her algae fertilizer won the grand prize at the International Science and Engineering Fair in 1979.

The fertilizer she developed is new, but it is based on an old idea. For generations, farmers in some parts of the Far East have been using algae to help plants grow. Nearly a thousand years ago a monk named Khong Minh Khong who lived near the mouth of the Red River in what is now Vietnam made an interesting discovery. The monks had to grow their own food, and the main crop then and now in that region is rice. It does well near the river, as it grows best in puddles of water that are known as "paddies." When Khong Minh Khong planted the floating water fern Azolla in the rice paddies near the monastery, the rice plants there grew better than they had before.

The farmers in the three villages nearby, La Van, Bung, and Bich Du, saw what was happening, and they quickly planted Azolla in their paddies, too, and got the same good results. They were so grateful to Khong Minh Khong that after he died they built temples to him on the banks of the Red River. The farmers of La Van, Bung, and Bich Du kept the secret of Azolla to themselves for many centuries, passing it down from father to son.

Khong Minh Khong, however, was not the only person to make this discovery. Three hundred years ago in another part of Vietnam there lived a peasant woman, Ba Heng. She tended the rice paddies for her family and also saw how the water fern helped the rice grow. The farmers in the nearby villages were

A farmer follows a centuries-old tradition for growing rice in a paddy, letting algae serve as a natural fertilizer.
(UNITED NATIONS.)

grateful to Ba Heng for teaching them about the water fern. Every fall from then to today a festival has been held in her honor.

But though Khong Minh Khong, Ba Heng, and the farmers knew that the fern helped the rice grow, they did not know how or why. And when twentieth-century botanists began to study the Azolla in the rice fields, they were surprised by what they learned. The fern did not really do much by itself. The rice plants were helped by the blue-green algae that live on the fern.

Down at the very bottom of the leaves of the Azolla are holes, and inside these holes, a kind of algae, Anabaena (pronounced anna-bee´-nah), is growing. The fern and the algae have a very close partnership. Each of them feeds the other. The fern gives the algae some of the substances they need for nourishment, and the algae give the fern some of the substances it needs. One of the most important of these is nitrogen. This chemical is used by all living things. The algae not only feed nitrogen to the fern, but have so much left over that they feed the rice plants as well.

It may seem odd that getting enough nitrogen would be a problem for a plant when we know that the air itself is mostly made up of nitrogen. But the rice cannot take the nitrogen from the air as is. For the nitrogen to do the plant any good, it first has to be combined with other substances and so become part of a chemical compound. The word used to describe this process is "fixing" nitrogen.

Unfortunately, rice, wheat, corn, and other plants cannot fix nitrogen. The only forms of life that can take the nitrogen from the air and fix it in the soil or water are algae and bacteria. And so when Ba Heng and Khong Minh Khong put ferns into the rice paddies, the algae attached to the leaves fixed nitrogen and helped the rice plants grow. The poor farmers in the Far East who cannot afford to buy fertilizer can use algae instead, as Ba Heng did.

Millions of people are saved from starvation because these algae make the rice crops bigger. While you probably eat rice only once in a while, it is the main food for people living in Vietnam, China, Japan, India, and most of the rest of the tropical world. Algae are very important in this area because they can not only be used as food by themselves, but also help other food crops grow better.

But as time passed and farming experts traveled through the tropics, they discovered something puzzling. Some rice growers who were not adding any algae to their paddies were getting larger crops than farmers nearby. The scientists were sure that they would find that the water fern and its algae had found their way into these paddies by themselves. But no matter how carefully they searched, they could find no trace of either the fern or the Anabaena.

They took this problem to the International Rice Research Institute (IRRI), which has its headquarters in the Philippines and works to improve rice production all over the world. The experts there soon found that Anabaena were not the only algae that could help the rice plants grow. In fact, botanists on the IRRI staff discovered at least 125 different kinds of algae that could fix nitrogen.

Most were not in partnership with a fern or other plant. Some formed a scum over the puddle just as they do over a stagnant pond, and others made a crust on top of the mud.

The next step was to work out a way of adding some of these algae to paddies where rice crops were small. The All India Coordinated Project of Algae made up a particularly good recipe using six kinds of algae. Then it set up an algae school for farmers where they learned how to grow the algae to add to their fields. Enough algae could be grown in just one fairly small tray in only two or three months to fertilize a rice farm of two and a half thousand acres.

The paddies with algae added gave fifteen percent more rice than paddies that were left alone.

But the system does not always work. Sometimes the good algae are forced out of the paddy by other, hardier, species that don't fix nitrogen. And one year fish invaded the rice paddies around Lake George in Uganda, Africa, and ate up all the algae. In India one summer the algae in some of the paddies suddenly disappeared. When the farmers strained the water to find out why, they found that it was filled with tiny water fleas. The fleas were very healthy because they had eaten all the algae. It had taken them only two weeks to do so.

The fact that algae can fix nitrogen when they are not being attacked by fleas and fish is important to many plants in addition to rice. Botanists often wondered how plants could live in coral reefs. When Robert H. Burris of the University of Wisconsin studied the reefs of Lizard Island on the Great Barrier Reef near Cooktown, Australia, he was struck by the harsh conditions there. When the tide is high, the waves beat against the reefs, hitting them with water, sand, and pebbles. Then it sweeps out, leaving the reefs high and dry beneath the merciless sun.

Yet not only the coral, which are tiny animals, but many tiny plants cling to life on the reef. There is no way of putting fertilizer on the coral reefs, and yet somehow the plants get enough nitrogen to survive. This is possible, suggests Burris, because blue-green algae also grow on the coral. They fix the nitrogen from the air to make life possible for corals, anemones, and other microscopic sea animals and plants.

Though algae love water, they can put up with weeks and months without rain. In Senegal, Africa, the dry season lasts about eight months. At the end of that time, most plants are dead. Ninety-five percent of those that survive each year are blue-green algae. Without these algae, the soil would not be rich enough to grow crops when the rainy season comes again.

"I've changed my luck," says a farmer. "Every year during the dry season I travel miles to find a lake where algae grow. I gather them and carry them back to put in the puddles that form on my farm when the rain starts to fall. The land is so poor at the start that you would think nothing could grow. But after the algae have been there, I can plant my seeds."

Algae are nature's own nitrogen fertilizer.

In 1883 a volcano erupted on the tiny Indonesian island of Krakatoa. It covered the entire island with hot molten rock, lava. This poured from the mountain, killing plants and animals. The natives of the island fled. Time passed and the lava cooled and the people came back to stand at what used to be their fields, shaking their heads sadly at the burned-out land, sure that no plant could have survived the catastrophe. But then a farmer noticed that a thin green crust had formed over the volcanic soil. He didn't think much of its looks and went away discouraged.

But he was discouraged too soon. Years went by and this green crust grew and spread farther over the island. As the algae took nitrogen from the air, the soil became darker and richer. The winds blew seeds onto the island. Finding nourishment there, a few small

A volcano erupts. When the lava cools, algae are the first form of life to appear. (U.S. AIR FORCE.)

plants began to poke their stems above the surface. In time Krakatoa was again covered with lush tropical plants and the volcano became the subject of stories told to the children at bedtime. None of the stories told of the wonderful green crust, though that would have been the best story of all.

The green crust of algae had added enough nitrogen to the soil for flowers, crops, trees, and hanging vines to flourish. In this way algae had helped to save the island.

10

A Strange and Useful Plant

One day the workmen taking care of ponds in California where algae were being grown saw a strange sight. A gas was rising from the bottom. They went back to the laboratory and asked the scientists what was happening.

The explanation lay in the algae. As some of the cells grew old and died, they dropped to the mud, and tiny organisms, fungi (pronounced fun'-jye) and bacteria, fastened on to them and made them decay. When any living thing decays, a gas is formed. This is known as methane or marsh gas, and it is a natural gas. Methane had long been known as a fuel, but no one had thought of using algae to make it.

Not only the tiny algae in the ponds but the giant kelp growing wild in the California coastal waters could produce this natural gas. Getting energy from algae is so appealing an idea that scientists in laboratories near the seacoast of New York decided there was no need to stay with the hot-climate algae that were being used in California. They would develop a system using the seaweeds that grow naturally in the cold, salty seawaters off Long Island. They took nine species of seaweeds and put them out on small rafts. Then they picked out the three that made the most methane and were the least bothered by the winter storms.

While watching the seaweeds, scientists were also looking for a good place to put a seaweed farm, says Jeffrey M. Peterson of the New York State Energy Research and Development Authority. The farm would have to be anchored to the sea bottom with ropes.

We will not soon be using algae power to turn on the lights, heat houses, and make cars go. Algae for energy is still a new idea, and it has not yet been fully worked out. But someday, as the ordinary fuels we burn today become scarcer and probably more expensive, algae power may come into its own.

Walter H. Adey of the Smithsonian Institution in Washington has suggested another way of producing fuel, and possibly food, by growing algae on a much bigger scale. He sees a series of floating platforms set out in the tropical seas. Encouraged by the brilliant sunlight, the algae would flourish on the platforms. They would be harvested and used to make fuel. Crabs, nourished by the algae and harvested as food, could be a second crop. Model platforms in the form of rectangular boxes have been built; on the bottoms are plastic screens on which the algae are grown. They are lit from above by electric light in the Smithsonian laboratory, by the sun at sea.

The algae platforms will not bring pollution to the waters of the world, but will instead make them cleaner. Algae are able to clean up not only water that

A plan to create algae farms on floating platforms begins with an experiment at the Smithsonian. Algae are being grown under laboratory conditions duplicating those of the tropical seas. (TIM GOERTMILLER/SMITHSONIAN INSTITUTION.)

has sewage in it, but also water that is polluted by wastes from factories.

Every month Japanese government officials pick a clump of seaweed that grows in the shallow waters of the bay near the tiny village of Urazoko. A nuclear-power plant was recently built near this spot. The officials check the seaweed to find out if radiation is leaking from the power plant. Certain species of algae take radioactivity from the water into their cells and the amount can be measured. On one of the monthly check-ups the Japanese found the seaweeds had suddenly become more radioactive. Engineers rushed to the plant and discovered that there had been a small leak.

Algae can also be used to discover that a body of water is becoming polluted—and not only by radiation. To find out what is happening to a river or lake, workers gather a bunch of seaweeds and ask a botanist to identify them. The kinds of seaweed present show the kind of pollution present. Certain species simply stop growing in polluted waters, while others like the pollution and grow even better. By now the botanists know which algae are which. When a factory was built in Maryland, a Chlorella strain in a nearby bay began growing and multiplying, while some of the other tiny plankton just died out. In England, botanists have noticed that the sea lettuce grows best when there is sewage in the water.

There seems to be no end to the uses for algae. Some

are very old, and others are only now being discovered. Seaweed comes in many colors, and so people living near the sea have had the idea of making dyes out of them. The royal purple that was popular in ancient Rome was taken from seaweed of that color. The Roman women of the time made their lips and cheeks look brighter with red and pink algae lipstick and blusher. The Eskimos also liked to give their faces color by rubbing on a red dye from seaweed, but they mixed it with fish oil first. You might not think much of the smell, but the Eskimos did not mind, and the oil protected their skin from the cold.

Some kinds of algae do have a pleasing grassy, mossy, or ocean smell, and this, too, has been put to good use. "We take 'absolute algae' from seaweed," says a perfume maker. "This is the part of the algae that smells. We need an awful lot of seaweed to get just a little of this, but it's worth the trouble."

Many other chemicals come from algae, too. In Israel not long ago scientists gathered a tiny red algae species growing in a salt marsh on the Sinai coast. Back in the laboratory, they found that this simple alga has in it the chemical glycerol, which is usually made from expensive petroleum. Glycerol is used in foods and cosmetics and to make other valuable chemicals. The scientists also discovered that the algae's color was due to carotene, another chemical in the cell. This is the same coloring you see in carrots, and it is sometimes added to foods to make them a prettier color. Carotene is a good source of vitamin A, too.

Nowadays, doctors have a large number of medicines to prescribe, and new ones are continually being developed in modern laboratories. In the old days doctors did not have a big choice. They had to find medicines by themselves. And so they looked to the plants around them. Over the years they discovered that certain plants really did help to make sick people well.

In India many hundreds of years ago seaweed was gathered from the rivers, and patients with neck swellings were told to eat it. The swellings went down. Today we know that swelling as goiter, a symptom of a disease of the thyroid gland, and it is treated with iodine. Seaweed has iodine in it; that is why the old Indian method worked. Doctors in ancient China often gave their patients a bit of "dragon's tongue," their nickname for a common seaweed.

During the Middle Ages monks had the role of helping the sick. They prescribed algae to relieve stomachaches. The recipe has come down to us: Boil the seaweed until it forms a jelly, then add spicy ginger and sugar to give it a good taste. Algae are still used in many medicines for upset stomachs. Sometime when you are in a drugstore, take a look at the stomach pills and powders on the shelf. On each package in tiny print is a list of ingredients, and on many of these lists you'll find such substances as alginic acid or agar. These come from seaweed. The algae help to make a medicine smooth and give it a nice feeling in the mouth. That's one of the reasons algae are added to ice creams and puddings as well as medicine.

Another recipe has come down to us from the monks: Heat algae, dry them, and mix in enough milk to make a paste; then add some sugar and spice. The monks ate the paste to help them keep active during heat waves. Nowadays we are sometimes advised to put extra salt on our food during heat waves, because we lose so much salt in sweat. And this loss makes us weak. Seaweeds coming out of the salty sea are very salty, too. That's why the paste made the monks feel better in the heat.

Because algae are so healthful and grow so freely, they have saved the lives of many people lost in barren regions. The Bible tells that when the Israelites left Egypt and were starving in the wilderness, a food, manna, was provided and kept them alive during the forty years of their journey. Manna was described as a "flake-like thing" lying on the ground. The Israelites gathered the manna and baked it into a bread.

Over the centuries botanists have tried to figure out what kind of plant manna might have been, and many of them believe that it was a lichen. This plant (pronounced lye'-ken) is one of the strangest on earth, made up of two completely different organisms. One of them is an alga, the other a fungus. And together they look like a "scale" or crust over the ground.

You may wonder why such a plant exists. Though algae have been found in hot regions and cold, in the sea and on land, there are some places where conditions are so harsh that even algae cannot do well. They may survive, but they are few in number. And so they have gone into partnership with another simple form of life. This combination plant can live because the fungi partners take water and chemicals out of air and rock that are almost dry. The fungi give the water and chemicals to the algae, which use them to perform photosynthesis, grow, and multiply. The fungi then can draw their food out of some of the algal cells. Together these simple organisms can stand anything. We can never be certain that lichens were the biblical manna, but in parts of the Arctic they are the only plant food for caribou and reindeer. In places where food is really scarce, people eat lichens, too. Like the manna, lichens can be ground into a flour and baked into bread.

Algae will always find a way of getting by in a hard world. In order to do so, they may take up with some very unusual partners, in addition to the fungus. An even more surprising partnership than the lichen has been set up with a tiny insect in the Antarctic. Both the algae and the insect live on the bottoms of the rocks in the ice-free valleys. Having nothing else to eat, the insect eats the algae. You might think this would be the end of the story, but not for algae. They are so hardy that they live on in the digestive system of the insect. Some can survive the digestive process. After a while the insect gets rid of the algae. As soon as they are out in the open again, they quickly recover and begin to grow and to reproduce until there are enough to feed some more insects.

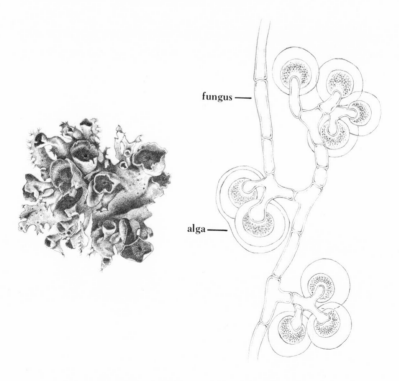

A perfect partnership between an alga and a fungus creates the hardy lichen plant.

But the insect is helping the algae, too. By themselves algae cannot move, and there is little water for them to use, and few chemicals in the soil in any one spot in the very cold, dry Antarctic. So they travel inside the insect's body as if in an airplane cabin and go to new places where conditions for life are better.

In these many ways algae have survived through the ages. The simplest of all plants existing today, they are the oldest: old when the first ferns grew in the prehistoric tropical swamps, old when humans appeared on the earth. Some of their uses have been known for hundreds, even thousands of years. But others are new. Now we are coming to see that someday they might feed the hungry of the world, improve farmland, produce energy, and help in the conquest of space.

We should not be surprised that algae can do so much. They have been around for more than three billion years—giving oxygen, offering food, and making this a more comfortable world for us to live in.

**Giant kelp
(Macrocystis)**

Index